How to Start a Service Business

A Step By Step Guide To Starting a New Small Service Company

I0474849

By Meir Liraz

Published by BizMove
www.bizmove.com

ISBN: 9781090313300

Table of Contents

c. How to Improve Your Leadership and Management Skills (eBook) - Discover powerful strategies to motivate and inspire your people to bring out the best in them. Be the boss people want to give 200 percent for.

d. Small Business Management: Essential Ingredients for Success (eBook) - Learn effective business management tricks, secrets and shortcuts to make your business a success.

1. Things to Consider Before You Start

This guide will walk you step by step through all the essential phases of starting a successful service business. To profit in a service based business, you need to consider the following questions: What business am I in? What services do I provide? Where is my market? Who will buy? Who is my competition? What is my sales strategy? What merchandising methods will I use? How much money is needed to operate my firm? How will I get the work done? What management controls are needed? How can they be carried out? When should I revise my plan? And many more.

No one can answer such questions for you. As the owner-manager you have to answer them and draw up your business plan. The pages of this guide are a combination of text and workspaces so you can write in the information you gather in developing your business plan - a logical progression from a commonsense starting point to a commonsense ending point.

It takes time and energy and patience to draw up a satisfactory business plan. Use this Guide to get your ideas and the supporting facts down on paper. And, above all, make changes in your plan on these pages as that plan unfolds and you see the need for changes.

Bear in mind that anything you leave out of the picture will create an additional cost, or drain on your money, when it crops up later on. If you leave out or ignore enough items, your business is headed for disaster.

Keep in mind too, that your final goal is to put your plan into action. More will be said about this near the end of this Guide.

What's in this for Me?

You may be thinking: Why should I spend my time drawing up a business plan? What's in it for me? If you've never drawn up a plan, you are right in wanting to hear about the possible benefits before you do your work.

A business plan offers at least four benefits. You may find others as you make and use such a plan. The four are:

(1) The first, and most important, benefit is that a plan gives you a path to follow. A plan makes the future what you want it to be. A plan with goals and action steps allows you to guide your business through turbulent economic seas and into harbors of your choice. The alternative is drifting into "any old port in a storm."

(2) A plan makes it easy to let your banker in on the action. By reading, or hearing, the details of your

plan he will have real insight into your situation if he is to lend you money.

(3) A plan can be a communications tool when you need to orient sales personnel, suppliers, and others about your operations and goals.

(4) A plan can help you develop as a manager. It can give you practice in thinking about competitive conditions, promotional opportunities, and situation that seem to be advantageous to your business. Such practice over a period of time can help increase an owner-manager's ability to make judgments.

Why am I in Business?

Many enterprising people are drawn into starting their own business by the possibilities of making money and being their own boss. But the long hours, hard work, and responsibilities of being the boss quickly dispel and preconceived glamour.

Profit is the reward for satisfying consumer needs. But it must be worked for. Sometimes a new business might need two years before it shows a profit. So where, then, are reasons for having your own business?

Every business owner-manager will have his or her own individual reasons for being in business. For some, satisfaction come from serving their community. They take pride in serving their neighbors and giving them quality work which they stand behind. For others, their business offers them a chance to contribute to their employees' financial security.

There are as many rewards and reasons for being in business as there are business owners. Why are you in business?

_____

_____

_____

What business am I in?

In making your business plan, the first question to consider is: What business am I really in. At the first reading this question may seem silly. "If there is one thing I know," you say to yourself, "it is what business I'm in." But hold on. Some owner-managers go broke and others waste their saving because they are confused about the business they are in.

The changeover of barbershops from cutting hair to styling hair is one example of thinking about what business you're really in.

Consider this example, also. Joe Riley had a small radio and TV store. He thought of his business as a retail store though he also serviced and repaired anything he sold. As his suburb grew, appliance stores emerged and cut heavily into his sales. However, there was an increased call for quality repair work.

When Mr. Riley considered his situation, he decided that he was in the repair business. As a result of thinking about what business he was really in, he profitably built up his repair business and has a contract to take care of the servicing and repair business for one of the appliance stores.

Decide what business you are in and write your answer in the following spaces. To help you decide, think of the answers to questions such as: What inventory of parts and materials must you keep on hand? What services do you offer? What services do people ask for that you do not offer? What is it you are trying to do better, more of, or differently from your competitors?

_____

2. How to Plan Your Marketing

When you have decided what business you're in, you have made your first marketing decision. Now you are ready for other important considerations.

Successful marketing starts with the owner-manager. You have to know your service and the needs of your customers.

The narrative and work blocks that follow are designed to help you work out a marketing plan for your firm. The blocks are divided into three sections:

Section One - Determining the Sales Potential

Section Two - Attracting Customers

Section Three - Selling to Customers

Section One - Determining the Sales Potential

In the service business, your sales potential will depend on the area you serve. That is, how many customers in this area will need your services? Will your customers be industrial, commercial, consumer, or all of these?

When picking a site to locate your business, consider the nature of your service. If you pick up and deliver, you will want a site where the travel time will be low and you may later install a radio dispatch system. Or, if the customer must come to your place of business, the site must be conveniently located and easy to find.

You must pick the site that offers the best possibilities of being profitable. The following questions will help you think through this problem.

In selecting an area to serve, consider the following:

Population and its growth potential

Income, age, occupation of population

Number of competitive services in and around your proposed location

Local ordinances and zoning regulations

Type of trading area (commercial, industrial, residential, seasonal)

For additional help in choosing an area, you might try the local chamber of commerce and the manufacturer and distributor of any equipment and supplies you will be using.

You will want to consider the next list of questions in picking the specific site for your business:

Will the customer come to your place of business?

How much space do you need?

Will you want to expand later on?

Do you need any special features required in lighting, heating, ventilation?

Is parking available?

Is public transportation available?

Is the location conducive to drop-in customers?

Will you pick up and deliver?

Will travel time be excessive?

Will you prorate travel time to service call?

Would a location close to an expressway or main artery cut down on travel time?

If you choose a remote location, will savings in rent off-set the inconvenience?

If you choose a remote location, will you have to pay as much as you save in rent for advertising to make your service known?

If you choose a remote location, will the customer be able to readily locate your business?

Will the supply of labor be adequate and the necessary skills available?

What are the zoning regulations of the area?

Will there be adequate fire and police protection?

Will crime insurance be needed and be available at a reasonable rate?

I plan to locate in _____ because:

_____

_____

_____

Is the area in which you plan to locate supported by a strong economic base? For example, are nearby industries working full time? Only part time? Did any industries go out of business in the past several months? Are new industries scheduled to open in the next several months?

Write your opinion of the area's economic base and your reason for that opinion here.:

_____

_____

Will you build? _____ What are the terms of the loan or mortgage?

_____

_____

Will you rent? _____ What are the terms of the lease?

_____

_____

Is the building attractive? _____ In good repair? _____

Will it need remodeling? _____ Cost of remodeling? _____

What services does the landlord provide?

_____

_____

What is the competition in the area you have picked?

The number of firms that handle my service

_____

Does the area appear to be saturated? _____

How many of these firms look prosperous?

_____

Do they have any apparent advantages over you?

_____

How many look as though they're barely getting by?

_____

How many similar services went out of business in the area last year? _____

Can you find out why they failed? _____

How many new services opened up in the last year? _____

How much do your competitors charge for your service? _____

Which firm or firms in the area will be your biggest competition? _____

List the reasons for your opinion here:

_____

_____

Section Two - Attracting Customers

When you have a location in mind, you should work through another aspect of marketing. How will you attract customers to your business? How will you pull customers away from your competition?

It is working with this aspect of marketing that many service firms find competitive advantages. The ideas which they develop are as good and often better, than those which large companies develop with hired brains. The workblocks that follow are designed to help you think about image, pricing, customer service policies, and advertising.

Image

Whether you like it or not, your service business is going to have an image. The way people think of your firm will be influenced by the way you conduct your business. If people come to your place of business for your service, the cleanliness of the floors, the manner in which they are treated, and the quality of your work will help form your image. If you take your service to the customer, the conduct of your employees will influence your image. Pleasant, prompt, courteous service before and after the sale will help make satisfied customers your best form of advertising.

Thus, you can control your image, Whatever image you seek to develop. It should be concrete enough to promote in your advertising. For example, "service with a smile" is an often used image.

Write out what image you want customers to have of your business.

_____

_____

Pricing

In setting prices for your service, there are four main elements you must consider:

(1) Materials and supplies

(2) Labor and operating expenses

(3) Planned profit

(4) Competition

Further along in this Guide you will have the opportunity to figure out the specifics of materials, supplies, labor, and operating expenses. From there you may want the assistance of your accountant in developing a price structure that will not only be fair to the customer, but also fair to yourself. This means that not only must you cover all expenses but also allow enough margin to pay yourself a salary.

One other thing to consider. Will you offer credit? _____ Most businesses use a credit card system. These credit costs have to come from somewhere. Plan for them. If you use a credit card system, what will it cost you? _____

Can you add to your prices to absorb this cost?

Some trade association have a schedule for service charges. It would be a good idea to check with the trade association for your line of business. Their figures will make a good yardstick to make sure your prices are competitive.

And, of course, your prices must be competitive. You've already found out your competitors' prices. Keep these in mind when you are working with your accountant. If you will not be able to make an adequate return, now is the time to find out.

Customer Service Policies

Customers expect certain services or conveniences, for example, parking. These services may be free to the customer, but not to you. If you do provide parking, you either pay for your own lot or pick up your part of the cost of a lot which you share with other businesses. Since these conveniences will be an expense, plan for them.

List the services that your competitors provide to customers:

_____

_____

_____

Now list the services that you will provide your customers:

Service / Estimated Cost

_____ _____

_____ _____

_____ _____

_____ _____

3. Planning Your Advertising Activities

In this section on attracting customers, advertising was saved until last because you have to have something to say before advertising can be effective. When you have an image, price range, and customers services, you are ready to tell prospective customers why they should use your services.

When the money you can spend on advertising is limited it is vital that your advertising be on target. Before you can think about how much money you can afford for advertising, take time to determine what jobs you want advertising to do for your business. The work blanks that follow should be helpful to your thinking.

The strong points about my service business are:

_____

My service business is different from my competition in the following ways:

_____

My advertising should tell customers and prospective customers the following facts about my business and services:

_____

When you have these facts in mind, you now need to determine who you are going to tell it to. Your advertising needs to be aimed at a target audience - those people who are most likely to use your services. In the space
below, describe your customers in terms of age, sex, occupation, and whatever else is necessary depending on the nature of your business. This is your customer profile of "male and female automobile owners, 18 years old and above." Thus, for this repair business, anyone over 18 who owns a car is likely to need its service.

The customer profile for my business is

_____

Now you are ready to think about the form your advertising should take and its cost. You are looking for the most effective means to tell your story to those most likely to use your service. Ask the local media (newspapers, radio and television, and the printers of direct mail pieces) for information about the services and the results they offer for your money.

How you spend advertising money is your decision, but don't fall into the trap that snares many advertisers. As one consultant describes this pitfall: It is amazing the way many managers consider themselves experts on advertising copy and media selection without any experience in these areas.

The following blanks should be useful in determining what advertising is needed to sell your strong points to prospective customers.

Form of Advertising	Size of Audience	Frequency of Use	Cost of A Single Ad	Estimated Cost
_____	_____	_____	_____	_____
_____	_____	_____	_____	_____
_____	_____	_____	_____	_____
_____	_____	_____	_____	_____
			Total	_____

When you have a figure on what your advertising for the next 12 months will cost, check it against one of the operating ratios (expenses as a percentage of sales) which trade associations and other organizations gather. If your estimated cost for advertising is substantially higher than this average for your line of service, take a second look. No single expense item should be allowed to get way out of line if you want to make a profit. Your task in determining comes down to: How much can I afford to spend and still do the job that needs to be done?

Section Three - Selling to Customers

To complete your work on marketing, you need to think about what you want to happen after you get a customer. Your goal is to provide your service, satisfy customers, and put money into the cash register.

One-time customers can't do the job. You need repeat customers to build a profitable annual sales volume. When someone returns for your service, it is probably because he was satisfied by his previous experience. Satisfied customers are the best form of advertising.

If you previously decided to work only for cash, take a hard look at your decision. Americans like to buy on credit. Often a credit card, or other system of credit and collections, is needed to attract and hold customers.

Based on this description and the dollar amount of business you indicated that you intend to do this year, fill in the following workblocks.

Fixtures and Equipment

No matter whether or not customers will come to your place of business, there will be certain equipment and furniture you will need in your place of business which will allow you to perform your service.

Parts and Material

You will probably need some kind of parts or material to provide your service.

I plan to buy parts and material from:

_____

Before you make any supply arrangements, examine the supplier's obsolescence policy. This can be a vital factor in service parts purchasing. You also look at the supplier's warranty policy.

Now that you have determined the parts and materials you'll need. you should think about the type of stock control system you'll use. A stock control system should enable you to determine what needs to be ordered on the basis of: (1) what is on hand, (2) what is on order, (3) what has been used. (Some trade associations and suppliers provide systems to members and customers.)

When you have decided on a system for stock control, estimate its cost. My system for stock control will cost me _____ for the first year.

Overhead

List the overhead items which will be needed. Examples are: rent, utilities, office help, insurance, interest, telephone, postage, accountant, payroll taxes, and licenses or other local taxes. If you plan to hire others to help you manage, their salaries should be listed as overhead.

_____

Getting the Work Done

An important step in setting up your business is to find and hire capable employees. Then you must train them to work together to get the job done. Obviously, organization is needed if your business is to produce what you expect it to produce, namely profits.

Organization is essential because you as the owner-manager cannot do all the work. As your organization grows, you have to delegate work, responsibility and authority. A helpful tool in getting this done is the organization chart. It shows at a glance who is responsible for the major activities of a business.

As an additional aid in determining both what needs to be done and who will do it, list each activity that is involved in your business. Next to the activity indicate who will do it. You may do this by name or some other designation such as "worker #1", Remember that a name may appear more than once.

Activity / Name

_____   _____

_____   _____

_____   _____

_____   _____

_____   _____

4. How Much Money Will You Need

At this point, take some time to think about what your business plan means in terms of dollars. This section is designed to help you put your plan into dollars.

The first question concerns the source of dollars. After your initial capital investment, the major source of money is the sale of your services. What dollar volume of business do you expect to do in the next 12 months? _____

Expenses

In connection with your annual dollar volume of business, you need to think about expenses. If, for example you plan to do 100,000 in business, what will it cost you to do this amount of servicing? And even more important, what will be left over as profit at the end of the year? Never lose sight of the fact that profit is your pay. Even if you pay yourself a salary for living expenses, your business must make a profit if it is to continue year after year and pay back the money you invested in it.

The following workblock is designed to help you make a quick estimate of your expenses. To use this formula, you need to get only one figure - the cost of sales figure for your line of business. If you don't have this operating ratio, check with your trade association.

	Expressed in percentage	Expressed in dollars	your percentage	your dollars
1. Sales	100	100,000	100	$ _____
2. Cost of sales	-61.7	-61,700	_____	-$ _____
3. Gross margin	38.3	38,300	_____	$ _____

Start-Up Costs

If you are starting a new business, list the following estimated start-up costs:

Fixtures and equipment	_____
Starting inventory	_____
Office supplies	_____
Decorating and remodeling	_____
Installation of equipment	_____
Deposits for utilities	_____
Legal and professional fees	_____
Licenses and permits	_____
Advertising for the opening	_____
Operating cash	_____
Owner's withdraw during prep-start-up time	_____
Total	_____

Whether you have the funds (savings) or borrow them, your new business will have to pay back these start-up costs. Keep this fact in mind as you work on the "Expenses" section, and on other financial aspects of your plan.

Break Down Your Expenses

Your quick estimate of expenses provides a starting point. The next step is to break down your expenses so they can be handled over the 12 months. Use an "Expenses Worksheet" form to make up an expense budget.

Matching Money and Expenses

A budget helps you to see the dollar amount of your expenses each month. Then from month to month the question is: Will sales bring in enough money to pay the firm's bills on time? The answer is "maybe not" or "I hope so" unless the owner-manager prepares for the "peaks and valleys" that are in many service operations.

A cash forecast is a management tool which can eliminate much of the anxiety that can plague you if your business goes through lean months. Use a worksheet, "Estimated Cash Forecast", or ask your accountant to use it to estimate the amounts of cash you expect to flow through your business during the next 12 months.

Is Additional Money needed?

Suppose at this point you have determined that your business plan needs more money than can be generated by sales. What do you do?

What you do depends on the situation. For example, the need may be for bank credit to tide your business over during the lean months. This loan can be repaid during the fat sales months when expenses are far less than sales. Adequate working capital is necessary for success and survival.

Whether an owner-manager seeks to borrow money for only a month or so or on a long-term basis, the lender needs to know whether the store's financial position is strong or weak. Your lender will ask to see a current balance sheet.

Even if you don't need to borrow, use it, to draw the "picture" of your firm's financial condition. Moreover, if you don't need to borrow money, you may want to show your plan to the bank that handles your store's checking account. It is never too early to build good relations with your banker, to show that you are a manager who knows where you want to go rather than a store owner who hopes to make a success.

Control and Feedback

To make your plan work you will need feedback. For example, the year-end profit and loss statement shows whether your business made a profit or loss for the past 12 months.

But you can't wait 12 months for the score. To keep your plan on target you need readings at frequent intervals. A profit and loss statement at the end of each month or at the end of each quarter is one type of frequent feedback. However, the income statement or profit and loss statement (P and L) may be more of a loss than a profit statement if you rely only on it. You must set up management controls which will help you to insure that the right things are being done from day to day and from week to week. In a new business, the record-keeping system should be set up before your business opens. After you're in business is too late. For one thing, you may be too busy to give a record-keeping system the proper attention.

The control system which you set up should give you information about: stock, sales, and disbursement. The simpler the system, the better. Its purpose is to give you current information. You are after facts with emphasis on trouble spots. Outside advisers, such as an accountant, can be helpful.

Stock Control

The purpose of controlling parts and materials inventory is to provide maximum service to your customers and to see that parts and materials are not lost through pilferage, shrinkage, errors, or waste. Your aim should be to achieve a high turnover on your inventory. The fewer dollars you tie up in inventory, the better.

In a business, inventory control helps the owner-manager to offer customers efficient service. The control system should enable you to determine what needs to be ordered on the basis of: (1) what is on hand, (2) what is on order, and (3) what has been used.

In setting up inventory controls, keep in mind that the cost of the inventory is not your only cost. You will also have costs such as the cost of purchasing, the cost of keeping control records, and the cost of receiving and storing your inventory.

Sales

In a small business, sales slips and cash register tapes give the owner-manager feedback at the end of each day. To keep on top of sales, you will need answers to questions such as: How many sales were made? What was the dollar amount? What credit terms were given to customers?

Disbursements

Your manager controls should also give you information about the dollars your company pays out. In checking on your bills, you do not want to know what major items, such as paying bills on time to get the supplier's discount, are being handled according to your policies. Your review system will also give you the opportunity to make judgments on the use of funds. In this manner, you can be on top of emergencies as well as routine situations.

Your system should also keep you aware that tax moneys such as payroll income tax deductions, are set aside and paid out at the proper time.

5. Break-Even Analysis

Break-even analysis is a management control device because the break-even point shows how much you must sell under given conditions in order to just cover your costs with No profit and No loss.

Profit depends on sales volume, selling price, and costs. Break-even analysis helps you to estimate what a change in one or more of these factors will do to your profits. To figure a break-even point, fixed costs, such as rent, must be separated from variable costs, such as the cost of sales and the other items listed under "controllable expenses" on the expense worksheet, of this Guide.

The formula is:

Break-even point (in sales dollars) =

$$\frac{\text{Total fixed costs}}{1 - \dfrac{\text{Total variable costs}}{\text{Corresponding sales volume}}}$$

An example of the formula is: Bill Jackson plans to open a laundry. He estimates his fixed expenses at about $9,000, the first year. He estimates his variable expenses at about $700 for every $1,000 of sales.

$$\text{BE point} = \frac{\$9{,}000}{1 - \dfrac{700}{1{,}000}} = \frac{\$9{,}000}{1 - .70} = \frac{\$9{,}000}{30} = \$30{,}000$$

Is Your Plan Workable?

Stop when you have worked out your break-even point. Whether the break-even point looks realistic or way off base, it is time to make sure that your plan is workable.

Take time to re-examine your plan before you back it with money. If the plan is not workable better to learn it now than to realize 6 months down the road that you are pouring money into a losing venture.

In reviewing your plan, look at the cost figures you drew up when you broke down your expenses for one year. If any of your cost items are too high or too low, change them. You can write your changes in the white spaces above or below your original entries on that worksheet. When you finish making your adjustments, you will have a Revised projected statement of sales and expenses for 12 months.

With your revised figures work out a revised break-even point. Whether the new break-even point looks good or bad, take one or more precaution. Show your plan to someone who has not been involved in working out the details.

Your banker, or other advisor outside of your business may see weaknesses that failed to appear as you pored over the details of your plan. They may put a finger on strong points which your plan should emphasize.

Put Your Plan into Action

When your plan is as near on target as possible, you are ready to put it into action. Keep in mind that action is the difference between a plan and a dream. If a plan is not acted upon, it is of no more value than a pleasant dream that evaporates over the breakfast coffee.

A successful owner-manager does not stop after he has gathered information and drawn up a plan, as you have done in working through this Guide. He begins to use his plan.

At this point, look back over your plan. Look for things that must be done to put your plan into action.

What needs to be done will depend on your situation. For example, if your business plan calls for an increase in sales, one action to be done will be providing funds for this expansion.

Have you more money to put into this business?

Do you borrow from friends and relatives? From your bank? From your suppliers by arranging liberal commercial credit terms.

If you are starting a new business, one action step may be to get a loan for fixtures, employee salaries, and other expenses. Another action step will be to find and hire capable employees.

In the spaces that follow, list things that must be done to put your plan into action. Give each item a date so that it can be done at the appropriate time. To put my plan into action, I must do the following:

Action / Completion Date

_____ _____

_____ _____

_____ _____

_____ _____

_____ _____

Keeping Your Plan Up To Date

Once you put your plan into action, look out for changes. They can cripple the best made business plan if the owner-manager lets them.

Stay on top of changing conditions and adjust your business plan accordingly.

Sometimes the change is made within your company. For example, several of your employees quit their jobs. Sometimes the change is with customers: for example, their desires and tastes shift. Sometimes the change is technological as when raw materials are put on the market introducing the need for new processes and procedures.

In order to adjust your plan to account for such changes, an owner-manager must:

(1) Be alert to the changes that come in your company, line of business, market, and customers.

(2) Check your plan against these changes.

(3) Determine what revisions, if any, are needed in your plan.

The method you use to keep your plan current so that your business can weather the forces of the market place is up to you. Read the trade papers and magazines for your line of business. Another suggestion concerns your time. Set some time - two hours, three hours, whatever is necessary-to review your plan periodically. Once each month, or every other month, go over your plan to see whether it needs adjusting. If revisions are needed, make them and put them into action.

6. How to Get New Customers

Finding New customers and more sales are essential for profit and growth. The business owner-manager should have a specific program for regularly developing new accounts. This Guide presents a systematic approach to finding, getting, and keeping customers whose sales volume produces profit for you.

The problem of finding new customers is a common one. A frequent lament of sales managers is "we just don't have enough new accounts to provide the volume we need." In most companies a five percent improvement in sales volume will have a most favorable profit effect. It will equal or exceed, for example, a comparable percentage improvement in costs of material and services, productivity, inventory management or control of receivables.

How to acquire the accounts to provide such added volume becomes a matter of prime importance to survival and growth. In a great many businesses, small and large, the matter of new customer acquisition is approached in a haphazard, intermittent, unplanned and uncoordinated way. The results are understandably often less than satisfying, more expensive than expected, and generally inadequate from the standpoint of contribution of profit.

Useful insight into the problem of getting new customers can be obtained by considering the sales department as a purchasing function, spending company resources by investing in customers and sales volume. The controls, systems, thought, and effort devoted to finding the right source of materials, providing for the most effective delivery performance at a favorable price, is a continuing and evident management concern relative to its purchasing activities. Disciplines are established and controls are in place to measure supplier and purchasing effectiveness. Alternate bids are secured and potential suppliers critically tested for quality and service. Capital expenditures are closely evaluated. Yet the problem of investing to get a new customer, one who is expected to deliver profitable sales over an extended period of time, is often reduced to a simple charge to the sales department of "more new customers!"

In most cases the investment in customer acquisition is heavy, scattered, unmeasured, and unplanned. The moneys spent in this type of effort consist of advertising dollars, sales salaries and expenses, phones, samples, administrative time, and often expensive engineering costs.

The alternative to the shotgun approach to new customer or account development is usually less expensive and substantially more productive. It involves some straightforward initial analysis and planning inexpensive enough for the smallest business. It may likewise involve a change in attitude and emphasis that says that the business of investing in a customer ought to be a selective, investigative, consistent, and planned process, worthy of the closest attention of the managing sales executive. Finding and developing a worthwhile customer is a different objective from simply "more sales" or "more accounts."

The procedure involves ten steps, formalized to the degree necessary for the needs of the enterprise. These are:

1. Specify

2. Quantify

3. Identify

4. Qualify

5. Convince

6. Service

7. Collect

8. Measure

9. Expand

10. Repeat

The first seven are initially critical. A substantial account that does not pay is no "customer."

Specify

The first step is to decide what kind of new customer is needed. This involves a brief customer "specification." No one just buys steel or a machine tool or a truck. The kind of steel, its characteristics, its yield are matters of instant concern. Are we trying to buy a simple drill press or a numerically controlled multiple spindle processing unit? Does the truck have to carry one ton or ten tons, and what is to be hauled? Good analysis of the strengths or deficiencies of your present customer accounts can help in preparing your customer specification.

The New Customer Specification Might Read:

Must be within 100 miles. Must be potentially capable of repeat purchases of product "x" totaling $50,000 per year. Must appreciate value of service as opposed to being strictly a price buyer. May be an intermittent process operation where downtime is a critical concern. Frequent changeovers. Quality conscious buyer. Pays promptly on terms. Probably in the Standard Industrial Classification (SIC) or , (describe)

May currently be using product supplied by National or Atlas. Size indicator: at least 100 employees, reasonable in-house maintenance program, evidence of sales growth. Objective: profit contribution rate of 30 percent.

Or the Specification Might Be Simply:

Companies in the meat processing industry, in Michigan, Ohio, Indiana, Kentucky, Pennsylvania (beef, lamb, pork, fowl) engaged in slaughter and/or portion pack, handling over 100 head/day equivalent;

Or:

Independent distributors of products associated with the material handling industry in major trading centers in the southeastern region, having a sales force of no less than five, and carrying recognized domestic truck brands calling on local industry, particularly food processors. Must have repair facilities.

Quantify

How many this quarter or this year? "To provide the type of business required, two new accounts with volume potential of $50,000 each are needed in each of the remaining quarters of the year, plus five new smaller customers in each quarter with a potential of $25,000 to $30,000 annually." Or, "Need an average of three new small machine accounts each territory, each quarter, with potential of supply sales of $2,500 each per year following installation."

Comment: The new account is admittedly a necessary consideration for growth. Some businesses, however, becomes so concerned with the new account syndrome that they overlook the very real, often untapped, potential of existing accounts. By proper attention to maintenance selling, accounts on the books can be upgraded, expanded to new applications, and in effect become new for all practical purposes. The maintenance aspect of selling is often minimized because the battle has been won - the customer is on the books. Neglect gives your competitors the opportunity to develop a new account by taking away one of your customers. In most cases, developing an existing account is much less costly than acquiring a new customer.

Identify

Having specified and quantified the type and number of new customers wanted, the next step is to identify and rough screen the most likely candidates in the most direct and least expensive way.

A few days devoted to secondary research can prove rewarding. The precise method depends on the scope of the project, the number of required new accounts and the geographic area involved.

For the smaller local business, the telephone directory is an obvious, available, and well organized reference for new accounts. In fact, a study of the directories for several cities provides a fast, comprehensive, and specific source of information for the significant trading centers in a region.

Such listings display products and services offered for sale, the nature of the services offered (like wholesaling, retailing, or manufacturing), the specific location, phone, and zip code reference. If the listings are regarded as definitive of what is sold, they likewise are definitive, with a little deduction, of what such firms buy for resale or as original equipment manufacturers, or for use in their businesses. For example:

Acme Rat Exterminating Products; Rentals, Service, Parts - Rat Poison, Roach Spray, Ant Bait, Bird Repellent, Rat Guards, Animal Traps, Chimney Screens, Sprayers (all types), Electric Fly and Mosquito Killers, etc., including map, address, phone, and brands handled.

Under "Mailing Lists" the yellow pages also give substantial listings of sources who provide listings of various types, often very specific as to

 Standard Industrial Classification (SIC) number, address, and names of relevant contacts. Purchase of one or more lists across the developed specification provides a fast way to be selective.

All things considered, like today's average cost of $100-$300 for an in-person industrial sales call, the time and money devoted to even modest preplanning data research is well spent.

Lists that can be bought generally key on SIC numbers that, depending on the number of classification digits, give names, size indicators, etc.

Other useful and readily available secondary sources of names are directories of associations, clubs, laboratories, manufacturer, Chamber of Commerce releases, mail order catalogs, and the like. The limit is only imposed by the extent of creative imagination of the researcher. The various desks in the federal and state offices and the public and university libraries are extremely helpful. Often license, permit, and registration data are available and useful.

Basic usage information to identify industries using forgings (by SIC number) was developed from a government report, "Census of Manufacturers." The scope of companies in those SIC groups was obtained for a specific geographic area from "County Business Patterns." A specific mailing list was then obtained from a directory publisher for specific SIC groups in those area. A rough screening of the list eliminated obvious unlikely prospects (Qualify). Two hundred phone calls were made to the remainder, asking the specific question, "How much do you buy of this type of forging?" Eighty-seven users were identified, large users were coded, and a program of selective selling on twenty-two accounts (some unsuspected users) was undertaken.

Qualify

One of the better sources of new customers among existing users of a product or service is your direct or indirect competitor.

Examination of the sales literature, catalogs, and trade releases of a competitor often reveals a pattern of distribution, a listing of good reference accounts, and often the details of best applications. Review of competitive advertising likewise points up many useful areas of concentration, selling methods, and coverage of what competitors regards to be their major markets.

Placing yourself in the role of a buyer of your own product or service is useful in identifying a competitor's influence points, likely user references, other applications that might not have occurred to you. Your own representatives can be helpful. In other words, shop around for your own product and see who else touches and end users in the distribution process. Each is a potential source of useful information. A frank discussion with some of your good customers will produce names of their competitors who might become your customers as well. Even on a limited local basis such efforts are most rewarding.

Your purchasing agent can be a most useful source of qualifying information because the agent talks to salesreps who talk to your competitors. In the field of selling, detailed attention to your competitors' activities can be as equally rewarding as attention to your own customers from the standpoint of identifying new customer opportunities, advantages, deficiencies, and needs. The cost is reasonable - an open eye or ear.

When the list is reasonable - identified, broadly qualified and manageable the personal contact or specific qualification phase begins. This takes time, but the effort will be spent on a modest group of targets that have been screened against your broad specification, qualified roughly at minimum cost and have a high probability of productivity.

Good mailing lists tied to selected group targets can help identify new accounts. By a proper offering (i.e., to conduct a free survey, to provide a sample, to solve a specific problem, to offer a study result, to provide a modest prize for best new application, etc.,) a user response can be obtained. From these responses you can qualify the potential of prospective new accounts.

Learning more about your end users can also uncover buyer habits and identifying characteristics indicative of a larger group. For instance, return warranty or registration cards could give you this information from comments or answers to a few basic questions about the product by users. This information can be matched to a larger group, expanding your viewpoint.

Look also for customers among users of alternative products or services to yours. For example, users of plastics are currently converting to die casting for various reasons. Gray iron castings can often be converted to stamped parts or forgings. Automobile buyers are acquiring motor bikes and supermarket shoppers are buying less at the store and eating out more at fast food restaurants. Such habits may bring back some lost customers or make you vulnerable to pressures from the indirect competition.

Convincing a potential user to try your product or service is the next step after you have found and qualified your prospects. This step is the pay off for all your efforts and investment to attract qualified customers. Convincing the potential user to try your product or service is often similar to qualifying customers according to your specifications.

You search in a specific market area for customers that are stable companies with solid needs for your products or services. They will do repeat business and pay their bills. And you are able to come to terms and do business with them.

Keeping customers involves giving service, getting paid, measuring account profitability, expanding customer buying, and then repeating all the steps to get and to keep good customer accounts.

Remember, treat old customers the way you service new ones and you may not need so many new ones.

The Profit Evaluation

How did you do against the measure you set for yourself? Is the trend better? Are your new customers delivering the quality of volume that you want? Tracking your progress is very important. Let's say you were shooting for no increase in fixed costs and $70,000 more profit contribution on the bottom line from new accounts.

There is more to getting new customers than just chasing the volume they produce. Obviously the quality of the volume is more important. Measure your required standard, not just for the amount, but for the profit yield of the volume and the trend for the future.

The new customer development method proposed here emphasized the who, what, why, when and where of volume rather than merely the how much. This takes thoughtful planning, detailed research and screening and some expense but you do get profitable results.

7. How To Set Optimal Prices

This guide discusses costing and setting prices of services to assure that each job earns a reasonable profit. The figures used in the tables and examples do not reflect what your service costs, set prices, and profits actually would or should be. The figures are used to demonstrate costing and set prices and are rounded off for further simplicity. Because of the importance and sometimes complexity of costing and pricing, it is good business practice to consult your trade association and particularly your accountant to learn what are the best current practices, cost ratios, and profit margins in your service business.

Setting Prices Problems

Many businesses are not making a profit today because they do not know the basic concepts of costing and set prices. The situation is most serious in the service business because each service performed has a different cost. Frequently, the service business must bid for jobs by making a price quotation in competition with similar businesses. Can you calculate your costs for your service and quote a price that is competitive and returns a profit?

Without realizing what they are doing, some business owners set their selling price below their total cost. This may result in more business for the company, but a loss will be incurred on each sale. Occasionally, a business owner who lacks a knowledge of costing will try to compensate by setting prices very high. The end result is that the business is not price competitive and does not attract sufficient customers to survive. Frequently, a business earns a profit on some particular service and loses money on other services without knowing which services are earning a profit and which services are incurring a loss. The year-end income statement combines the profits and losses from the various services performed over the year. Therefore, it is impossible to determine the profitability of specific service jobs from a year-end income statement.

Use a simplified approach to cost accounting that reflects the needs of the business and reports the cost with a reasonable degree of accuracy. The total cost of producing any service is composed of three parts: 1) the material cost, 2) the labor cost, and 3) the overhead cost. Direct materials and direct labor + overhead = total cost of service.

Cost Determination

Direct Material Cost

The direct material cost is made up of the cost to you for parts and supplies that are used on specific jobs. Once the list of parts and supplies to be used is developed, a check with the supplier will give an up-to-date material cost. The shipping and other handling (storage etc.) costs for the parts should be included in the material cost.

Direct Labor Cost

The direct labor costs include those labor costs identified with a specific service job. The labor cost involved in providing a service is determined by multiplying the number of direct labor hours required by the cost per direct labor hour. It is very important to determine accurately the amount of direct labor hours involved to complete the service; therefore, you must use a time clock, worksheet, or a daily time card for each employee to determine the exact amount of labor time spent on each service job.

The hourly cost of direct labor can be figured (priced) two ways. One it can be the hourly wage only, with fringe benefits, Social Security, Workers' Compensation, etc., (all labor-related costs) allocated to overhead. Or two, the hourly direct labor cost can include the hourly wage plus the employer's contribution to Social Security, unemployment compensation, disability, holidays and vacations, hospitalization and other fringe benefits (payroll costs).

By this second method, the added payroll costs for vacations, holidays and benefits are expressed as percentages of direct hourly wages. For instance, if two weeks of vacation and ten holidays are given annually, this amounts to four weeks per year or 7.7% (i.e., four weeks off divided by fifty-two weeks 4 : 52 = 7.7%) of total labor cost was for time off. Thus, to determine the total direct labor cost per hour by this method, you must add the prorated cost of the payroll taxes, worker's compensation, holidays and vacation pay, hospitalization, etc., to the hourly wage paid. As a rule of thumb, the sum of the various payroll-benefit costs have generally been in the range of 20% to 30% of the hourly wages paid. It is more complicated to figure but more precise to use the higher labor cost (including labor related labor costs). The following table shows a sample calculation for figuring the total direct labor cost using this more exact method.

ABC Repair Company

Table 1: Direct Labor Cost Calculation

(1) Hourly Wage	(2) Payroll Taxes @12%	(3) Workers Compensation @3%	(4) Total Direct Labor Cost Per Year*	(5) Vacation and Holiday Cost per Working Hour**	(6) Actual Direct Labor Cost per Working Hour***
8.04	.96	.24	19219.2	.57	9.87
9.78	1.17	.30	24400	.69	11.94
10.20	1.23	.30	24398.4	.72	12.45
10.86	1.29	.33	25958.4	.78	13.26
11.55	1.38	.36	27643.2	.84	14.13
12.30	1.47	.36	29390.4	.87	15.00
		Total	150,009.6		

*40 hrs/wk x 52 wks/yr = 2080 hrs/yr

**6.25% of Columns 1 + 2 + 3.

***Columns 1 + 2 + 3 + 5.

Overhead Cost

Overhead includes all job related costs other than direct materials and direct labor. Your overhead cost depends on which of the two ways you figured direct labor costs, with or without the labor-related payroll-benefits costs. If you did not include these expenses in direct labor, then you must include them in overhead. In our examples, however, these labor-related costs are included in direct labor and not in overhead. Either way the effect on the total job cost is the same, but your overhead cost varies accordingly.

Because they may not know how to allocate (or assign) overhead costs to the services performed, many business owner-managers miscalculate or avoid considering overhead costs.

Overhead is the indirect cost of the service and is made up of indirect materials, indirect labor, and other indirect costs related to particular services. Indirect materials are too minor to include as direct material costs. Incidental supplies and machine lubricants are examples. Indirect labor is the wages, salaries, and other payroll-benefit costs incurred by workers who do not perform the service but who support the main service function, such as, clerical, supply, and janitorial employees. Other costs, like taxes, depreciation, insurance, and transportation are also part of the overhead cost because the service cost includes a portion of all indirect costs (overhead). The following table projects total overhead for all services for one year. To figure the portion of overhead related to particular services or jobs, you allocate the various overhead costs by calculating the overhead rate.

The way you calculate the overhead rate should relate the overhead costs to the primary cause for the overhead cost being expended, reflecting a reasonable amount of total overhead to each service. The overhead rate can be expressed as a decimal, as a percentage, or as an hourly rate. The use of the overhead rate helps to assure that all the overhead costs expended throughout the year will be recovered as the business's services are sold throughout the year.

In a situation where employee wages vary a lot, as when higher paid employees work with more expensive equipment, the overhead cost is allocated on the basis of direct labor cost. This occurs because a large proportion of the overhead cost will consist of equipment depreciation (other indirect cost), interest on the capital invested in equipment, and electrical costs. The overhead rate is determined as follows:

(1) Overhead Rate =

$$\text{Overhead Rate} = \frac{\text{Total Overhead Cost}}{\text{Total Direct Labor Cost}}$$

This is the most common method for allocating overhead cost to the specific service performed. The above rate is suitable for machine shops and auto repair shops.

In some cases there is relatively little difference in the hourly wages paid to different employees. In other cases, no relationship exists between the level of the worker's skill and the amount of equipment used by the worker. Under such circumstances, total overhead cost may be allocated on the basis of direct labor hours as follows:

(2) Overhead Rate =

$$\text{Overhead Rate} = \frac{\text{Total Overhead Cost}}{\text{Total Direct Labor Hours}}$$

The above rate is suitable for businesses such as secretarial services or janitorial services. The overhead costs result mainly from the workspace, supervision, and electricity that the workers need in order to provide the service. Using formula (2), it is possible to determine the overhead cost per hour per employee.

Calculating the Overhead Cost

In determining the total overhead cost, a business should not depend solely on last year's income statement. Due to inflation and business growth, last year's overhead costs do not accurately reflect today's overhead cost. The best approach is to project the overhead costs for the near future, that is, the anticipated overhead expenses for the next six months to one year. The projected overhead cost will reflect additional administrative salaries, the depreciation of new equipment that the business plans to purchase, rent increases, energy cost increases, etc. Table 2 shows projected overhead expenses for a business, ABC Repair Company.

The payroll taxes included in the projected overhead expenses for the service business are only those paid on executive and office salaries. The direct labor payroll, taxes, holiday pay, vacation pay etc., are included in the direct labor cost shown in Table 1.

ABC Repair Company

Table 2: Projected Overhead Expenses for the upcoming year

Indirect Materials

Office Expenses	1,800
Postage	450
Repairs	2,900
Shop Supplies	2,700
Utilities	2,400
Telephone	4,400
	14,650

Indirect Labor

Executive Salaries	30,000
Office Salaries	7,000
Payroll Taxes	12,000
Travel & Entertainment	700
	49,700

Other Indirect Costs

Accounting	2,400
Advertising	4,800
Auto-Truck Expense	5,400
Depreciation	9,650
Insurance	1,240
Interest	2,560
Licenses	650
Miscellaneous Expense	500
Rent	8,450
	35,650

Total Overhead	100,000

To ensure that all overhead costs are included, it is best to project the overhead costs for a full fiscal year. This aids in the treatment of expenses that occur only once each year, such as business licenses.

Cost Calculation Example

Perhaps the most common type of service business is the repair business. The cost calculation procedure illustrated here for the repair business can be used for other types of service businesses. The only precaution that needs to be taken is that the appropriate overhead rate formula which reflects the business's operation, as discussed above, be used in the calculation.

It has been estimated, based upon previous experience, that a specific repair job will require $20 of parts and 2 hours of labor by an employee whose labor cost is $5.00 per hour. (These estimates will be used throughout this Guide.) As discussed earlier, the total cost of producing any service is composed of: 1) the material cost, 2) the labor cost, and 3) the overhead cost.

To determine the material cost (the cost of the parts), check the cost of the part in your inventory or get a price quote from your parts suppliers. A parts wholesaler is the source of the $20 material cost in this example.

To determine the total direct labor cost, the number of hours of direct labor used is multiplied by the actual direct labor cost per hour. An employee whose actual direct labor cost is $5.00 per hour, including payroll taxes and fringe benefits (see

Table 1), requires two hours to complete the repair job.

Labor Cost = Direct Labor Cost per Hour x Hours Required

Labor Cost = $5.00 per Hour x 2 Hours

Labor Cost = $10.00

The projected overhead expenses were projected to be $100,000 per year, as shown in Table 2. The nature of the repair business is that overhead costs are most directly related to direct labor costs than to direct material costs. The total projected direct labor cost including payroll taxes and fringe benefits was determined to be $50,003.20 (see Table 1). The formula selected to determine the overhead rate bases upon the direct labor cost is:

(1) Overhead Rate =

Total Overhead Cost

———————————————

Total Direct Labor Cost:

$100,000 : $50,003.20 = 2.00

In most small to medium businesses, the overhead rate is between one and two (i.e., between 100% and 200% of the direct labor cost). Businesses that are very labor intensive, such as a janitorial service, will have an overhead rate much less that 100%

To determine the overhead cost allocated to a specific job, the labor cost is multiplied by the overhead rate as shown below.

(1) Overhead Cost = Direct Labor Cost x Overhead Rate

$10.00 x 2.00 = $20.00

To determine the total cost of the repair job, the material cost, the direct labor cost, and the overhead cost are added together:

Material Cost	20.00
Direct Labor Cost	10.00
Overhead Cost	20.00
Total	50.00

How to Set Prices

Calculate the profit and add it to the total cost to get the price to charge for the service, in this case a repair job. Prices charged by competitors (similar service businesses), economic conditions of supply and demand, and legal, political, and consumer pressures all influence the profit you can expect for your service and hence the price you can charge for your jobs. Inflation, the amount of business you have (i.e., number of jobs), and your productivity (the efficiency and quality of your business and service) also all effect your profit and the way you figure your prices. You can choose from several pricing methods. Common business practice is to express profit as a percentage of the base used for pricing calculations no matter which pricing method you use.

Set Prices Alternatives

In considering the total cost of the repair job discussed above, the material cost can normally be predicted with a high degree of accuracy. Labor and overhead costs cannot be predicted with such a high degree of accuracy. An employee may not feel well on a given day. Or there may be an equipment breakdown. Either will result in higher than expected labor costs. A provision to adjust for fluctuating labor and overhead costs can be established through your approach to profit. The profit can be applied to the three costs independently, allowing for variations in labor and overhead costs among jobs. For example, a 10% profit on material, a 30% profit on direct labor, and a 30% profit on overhead can be used to determine the price of the service.

Material Cost + Profit of Material		
$20 +	$20 x 10%= $22.00	$2
Direct Labor Cost + Profit on Direct Labor		
$10 +	$10 x 30% = $13.00	$3
Overhead Cost + Profit on Overhead		
$20 +	$20 x 30%= $26.00	$6
────	────	────
$50 Cost	$61.00 Price	$11 Profit

The concept of applying a different rate of profit on the three underlying costs (material, labor, and overhead) is one method of dealing with the large difference in predictability of costs that exists between labor and materials in most service businesses. To reflect the fluctuations in utilization and cost of labor and overhead from job to job, your profit on labor and overhead should normally be higher than profits on materials.

Direct Cost Pricing

With this method you set your selling price based on direct cost, that is, on direct materials (DM) and direct labor (DL). DM of $20 plus DL of $10 equals Direct Costs of $30. Overhead (OH) costs are $20; so to earn the $11 profit you need, your selling price must be at least $31 above your direct cost to charge; divide direct costs into overhead plus needed profit:

$31 ($11 + $20) : $30 = 103 1/3\%$

(proof $30 x 103 1/3\% = $30 x 1.033 = $11)

In most small businesses, there is not a large amount of overhead cost associated with obtaining parts besides a telephone call to order them. Charging a large amount of overhead to parts may result in pricing yourself out of the market.

By all these methods you are deriving a selling price for your service. Sometimes however you start with the selling price already established - by competition or economic conditions. Then you must figure out the most cost you can incur and still earn your needed profit.

Setting Prices - Summary

The total cost of producing a service is composed of direct material, direct labor, and overhead costs. This cost information is used as a basis for setting prices and profit. From alternative pricing methods you select one that earns a satisfactory profit and is easy for you to use. Given regulations, competition, and the economy, you must have a pricing strategy that keeps your service competitive and profitable. The more exactly you figure your costs and set prices, the greater your chances for continued and profitable business.

8. Profitable Customer Relationship Management

Small Business Customer Satisfaction Loyalty - understanding and achieving Customer Satisfaction Loyalty - is essential for commercial success. This guide explains how small companies can profit from understanding their customers.

Understanding one's customers is so important that large corporations spend hundreds of millions annually on market research. Although such formal research is important, a small firm can usually avoid this expense. Typically, the owner or manager of a small concern knows the customers personally. From this foundation, understanding of your customers can be built by a systematic effort. A comprehensive system for understanding is what Rudyard Kipling called his six honest serving men. "Their names are What and Why and When and How and Where and Who."

What Customer Satisfaction Loyalty

A seller characterizes what customers are buying as goods and services - toothpaste, drills, video games. cars. . . But understanding of buyers starts with the realization that they purchase benefits as well as products. Consumers don't select toothpaste. Instead. some will pay for a decay preventive. Some seek pleasant taste. Others want bright teeth. Or perhaps any formula at a bargain price will do.

Similarly, industrial purchasing agents are not really interested in drills. They want holes. They insist on quality appropriate for their purposes, reliable delivery when needed, safe operation, and reasonable prices.

Video games are fun. They are bought for home entertainment, family togetherness, development of personal dexterity, introduction to computers, among other satisfactions. Commercial customers include arcades, pizza parlors, and assorted enterprises. They benefit from a potential source of income, a means of attracting buyers to their premises, or perhaps a competitive move.

Similarly, cars are visible evidence of a person's wealth, reflection of life style, a private cabin for romance. Or they represent receipts from leases, means to pursue an occupation. . . Some people even buy cars for transportation.

You must find out, from their point of view, what customers are buying. The common names of products mean as little to them as the chemical names on the label of a proprietary drug. (A sick person's real need is safe. speedy relief.)

Understanding your customers enables you to profit by providing what buyers seeks - satisfaction.

Products change, but basic benefits like personal hygiene, attractiveness, safety, entertainment, and privacy endure. So do commercial purposes such as quests for competitive superiority or profitability.

Successful manufacturers and service establishments produce benefits for which customers are willing to pay. Successful wholesalers and retailers select offerings of such demanded benefits that they can resell at a profit. Successful businesspeople, in other words. understand the reason for their customers' buying decisions

Why Customer Relationship Management

The reason that customers buy is logical from their point of view. Understanding customers derives from this fundamental premise. Don't argue with taste.

Everybody is unique. Each person has individual pressures and criteria. Moreover, perceptions differ. The astute businessperson deduces and accepts the buying logic of customers and serves them accordingly.

To learn why customers buy can be quite difficult.

Some buyers hide their true motivations. In many cases the reasons are obscure to the buyers themselves. Most purchase decisions are multi-causal. Often, conflicts abound. A car buyer may want the roominess of a large vehicle and the fuel economy of a subcompact. The resolution of such mutually exclusive desires is usually indeterminate.

Sometimes the reasons why customers buy are trivial. If customers feel indifferent toward a product or store, the selection is apt to be happenstance. Perhaps several rival offerings meet all the conditions that a purchaser deems important. Consequently, minor factors govern. This explains the rationale of the consumer who chose a $ 22,000 car because its upholstery was most attractive. The point: Pay attention to details. They may be crucial to customers.

Often the best clues are the customers' actions. Shrewd businesspeople respect what people say, but pay special attention to what people do. More important than why customers buy is why former customers have taken their patronage elsewhere and why qualified buyers are not buying. What is now keeping them from buying?

Can this obstacle be surmounted? Businesspeople monitor competitive offerings and buyers' reactions to infer clues. Informal conversations may also reveal some reasons. Special offers may overcome resistance and boost profits.

All the time the manager must be careful to retain the company's regular customers. For instance, a specialty dress shop may try to widen its patronage through a new line at bargain prices. This move could disturb the store's usual patrons. They may take their trade to another store that caters exclusively to their social class.

Many of the dresses were bought for special occasions when projection of a genteel image was important to the customer. Understanding of customers includes awareness of the time of the purchase and use of the merchandise.

When

A seller must be ready when the buyer is, lest an opportunity be irretrievably lost. Customers buy when they want an offering and have the time and money to purchase it. Buying patterns can often be discerned from an analysis of customers and their purchases. For example, wants for many consumer goods and services are tied to customers' rites of passage. The following purchase occasions in the adult life cycle are typical:

1. Marriage, separation, divorce

2. Acquisition of a home

3. Change in employment or career

4. Graduate study; running for office

5. Health care, injury, illness

6. Pregnancy, nurture of children

7. Children enter school; graduate

8. Children leave home (for college or permanently)

9. Move to another area

10. Vacations; major social activities

11. Permanent retirement from work

12. Death of a family member.

Shrewd retailers keep track of such key buying events and gain a head start on making sales. Logs of birthdays and anniversaries are a case in point. Additional purchase occasions are impersonal. Seasonal factors include recurring holidays and weather changes. Among other favorable influences on purchases are start of the school year, semi-annual white sales, introduction of new models and clearance of old ones, special price concessions, and improvement in economic conditions or buyer's confidence.

Some of the latter factors also apply to manufacturers. Small plants work closely with their buyers' inventory managers and replenish stock at their reorder point. A current vogue is just-in-time delivery. Interactive computers make replenishment notices routine.

Many consumers have time for shopping only during offhours. in the evenings, and on weekends. The trend from a single breadwinner per family toward having all adults of a household engage in commercial employment has intensified this time peculiarity. Astute retailers adjust their hours, staffing, and availability of merchandise to customers' shopping convenience. Bartenders know that business booms on payday. Manufacturers profit from timing their offers to their customers' budgetary cycles. Thus, knowing when products are bought and used is a valuable facet of understanding customers.

Although a transaction may be concluded in a moment, most purchases actually entail a drawn-out process.

This process will be described in the next section which analyzes how customers buy.

How

Knowledge of how customers buy pays off in several ways. (1) Sellers can design their offerings to meet the exact needs of their buyers. (2) Sellers can influence decision makers at crucial steps of the buying process. (3) Sellers can lay the groundwork for repeat business.

Buying methods are best visualized as processes. Household purchases usually start when a consumer has a desire or a problem that an acquisition might satisfy or solve. Industrial purchases usually start when a user or a routine sets off a signal (requisition) for approval of a procurement.

People are diverse. Every consumer, every firm pursues a buying process of its own. Buying processes also depend on the significance of the product to the buyer and on other circumstances. Although buying processes are not uniform. some steps are common to most of them. The seller needs to know only these critical steps when he or she can affect the outcome of the buying decision.

Shrewd sellers delve into the behavioral milestones of purchasers. But for each very important customer the buying process should be diagrammed individually, showing names of influencers at each decision stage, elapsed time between stages, and any other pertinent information.

Perhaps a change in life style or a demonstration at a friend's house has caused this consumer to recognize the need for a personal computer. But lack of knowledge and the fear of a wrong decision may counteract this desire. The process continues, however, if advertisements and expected benefits persuade the consumer to act. Despite budgetary constraints and uncertainty about future needs, the consumer proceeds to compare stores and brands.

At this search and evaluation stage advice from present satisfied customers is especially influential. Make sure your customers are satisfied and favorably recommend your merchandise or service. To the contrary, poor shopping facilities or irritating personnel can sway the potential customer against making the purchase from you.

Sooner or later, further search does not seem worthwhile. If the positives still outweigh the negatives, the consumer picks a store and brand. The transaction itself is consummated quickly, assuming the wanted item is available. The satisfied customer makes recommendations to others and gives you his or her repeated, regular business.

Businesspeople can create sales by predisposing potential buyers to their product or store. Manufacturers can offer exclusive benefits in their goods, such as friendly relations, efficient operations, and easy manuals. Enticing advertisements help persuade prospects to visit a retail outlet and ask about a particular brand. Creative salespeople overcome the customer's objections and doubts and close the sale. Post-transaction service keeps the customer satisfied. Referrals usually follow.

Specific details are needed to track acquisition of something complex, say a computer. On the other hand, less detail is needed if the purchase is laundry detergent or some other staple with which the customer is less involved. In the latter case, depletion of the home inventory triggers a routine, leading directly to choice: the usually purchased brand. If the usual brand is out-of-stock or another brand is on sale. a substitute may be bought quickly. Brand comparisons follow or may be omitted.

Some products are bought when an emergency need for them arises. A physical examination and the filling of a prescription are urgent when sickness strikes. Arrangements for funerals follow immediately after the death of a family member. Umbrellas are in demand when it rains. An unexpected snow storm generates extra calls for tire chains, towing services, and car batteries. Often, convenient availability determines when these goods and services are purchased. And even if customers do have ample time to select merchandise, sellers who stand ready to supply wanted or expected brands are apt to gain preference and profit when shoppers decide where to buy.

People want options. Although convenient availability is the main buying criterion for many routine household products, savvy merchants stock a selection conforming to the diverse preferences of their patrons. Some people demand manufacturers' advertised brands. Resellers' brands are favored by others. On some classes of goods, generic brands have become popular in recent years. Moreover, many consumers seek occasional variety. Clearly the decision of which products to stock is important.

It is more important yet on shopping goods because buyers compare them before purchase. And it is most important on specialty goods, those preselected by brand name. If a store does not stock these uniquely wanted brands, a prospect will leave without buying. Whoever offers them on acceptable terms gains the sale.

Where

From a multitude of studies emerge different criteria for deciding where to shop. Most research on the subject agrees that store location is a major consideration, Stores usually draw most of their patronage from their surrounding neighborhood.

Savvy store managers make a special effort to understand the shopping-related motivations and preferences of local residents. New managers of fast-food units, for example, canvass nearby dwellings and introduce themselves to the households. Some supermarkets maintain consumer advisory boards to elicit suggestions and reactions. Other means of communication with customers include informal conversations at the store and suggestion boxes with interviews and awards.

Incidentally, complaints are an excellent guide for making store policies more amenable to customers. Personnel should be instructed to thank patrons for their comments. Prompt consideration, followed by a personal letter from the store manager, is highly desirable.

Location is extremely important to "captive" buyers. Exclusively franchised utilities, shops in isolated hotels. and cafeterias or automatic vending machines in factories are examples. At the opposite extreme, shoppers escape spatial restrictions by buying from mail-order firms or telephone solicitors.

Other patronage influences vary. They depend on the type of product. type of store, and the characteristics of the consumer. The offered assortment's perceived quality. depth, and breadth certainly are very important. along with price, This does not imply that all goods have to be top quality or all prices the lowest. Perceptions are decisive.

If quality seems high, some customers infer that prices are high too regardless of the facts. The important point is to understand customers and to provide what causes them to buy. For example, assurance of repair service weighs heavily with the worrier type of customer. A convenience-minded buyer is concerned with parking space or delivery service.

Of course, shoppers must be told that wanted goods and services are available. Advertising helps disseminate this information. So does a store's reputation for consistent policies of satisfying its customers.

Occasional promotions inject some excitement into the tedium of shopping. Some clients like to socialize, which can absorb much of an employee's time and may even annoy other buyers. Nevertheless, personnel should be friendly and helpful. Also influential, for some customers, is the apparent socio-economic level of other shoppers.

Personal affinity for other customers or for salespeople is a decisive factor in the success of party-selling, e.g., household goods and in-home selling (cosmetics). The choice of where to buy items requiring major outlays (securities, and insurance) often revolves around from whom to buy.

In selecting a retail store, many customers consider physical features. Layouts can invite or repel patronage. Motorists who are in a hurry, for instance, are apt to use a gasoline station at which business can be transacted quickly. Altogether, buyers perceive a mix of tangible and intangible factors that comprise a store's atmosphere. Accordingly, they either do or don't feel comfortable about shopping there.

To the casual observer, all supermarkets seem more or Hess alike, But. in fact, store managers can regulate many of the above-mentioned variables and thereby affect where shoppers buy. According to recent studies in several American cities, household buyers perceive supermarkets in their neighborhood as sufficiently different to determine their patronage preference. The four main types of supermarkets offer: (1) High quality at commensurate prices, (2) Lowest price level in the area, (3) Swift completion, (4) Friendly atmosphere. Each can profit by appealing to a different segment of buyers. the topic of the next section.

Who

Identification of customers and prospects makes effective targeting possible. Small business owners pride themselves on knowing their customers personally. In the industrial field, understanding of each major customer and buying influence is essential. When dealing with a large number of customers, however, individual familiarity is not feasible. Hence mass merchandisers and others in this situation group their customers, whose reactions to offerings are similar, into segments. Then they design a separate appropriate marketing program for each segment.

Strategies vary, A small firm might prosper by concentrating its resources on one segment. Because customers are volatile, the specializing firm is vulnerable to sudden change in its target segment's patronage. Hence some companies address several segments simultaneously. Although expensive, a strategy of employing different tactics for different segments can be quite profitable.

Other firms scatter offers to just anybody. They hope that segments will select themselves.

One basis for segmentation is geographic. Retail customers are apt to live or work in the store's vicinity. Industrial buyers tend to concentrate regionally. So do users of services. Intensive cultivation of local potential customers can be efficient and lucrative. Personal knowledge of local buyers and a shared community spirit help cement relations with these customers.

Segmentation is an art. All "honest serving men" - what, why, when, how, where, as well as who - can be the key to segmentation. Whatever the basis, each identified segment should have sufficient purchasing power to make a special effort commercially worthwhile. Accessibility is vital. How can the segment be reached? Are advertisements, telephone solicitations, or personal visits efficient? How about trade shows or personal contacts? The ideal segment is stable in purchase needs and loyalty, helping you fend off competition.

Besides segmentation, understanding of customers also requires insight into their buying roles. The buyer for a one-person household or one-person business is the initiator of the order, the decider, and the user. Even in this case, however, some outsiders are influential.

In larger households or businesses, these buying roles are usually played by separate individuals. It helps you to know who activates (requisitions) purchases, who exerts influence, who decides what and where to buy, who uses the product-and what their criteria are. Then you tailor and target your offerings to satisfy each major participant in the buying process.

As has been shown, understanding of customers enables a seller to increase sales. This same understanding can equally serve to reduce costs. Higher sales at lower costs inevitably boost profits.

A small firm that understands its customers can buy or produce exactly what they want-and nothing else. The firm's sales effort is efficient because it builds on why its customers want to buy not on why others buy, or why the vendor wants to sell.

Merchandise can be ready when customers need it. Thus a knowledgeable seller avoids unnecessary inventory costs or penalties for late delivery. Understanding how customers buy lets a seller employ promotional media, appeals, and timing for maximum effectiveness. Transportation costs are lowered by shipping merchandise to where it is needed. Knowledge of who comprises suitable segments and the separate buying roles can reduce the waste of soliciting unqualified or uninterested people.

Customers Are Dynamic

The best source for you to learn about customers is your personal interaction with them. At work, social and civic activities, and chance encounters, people talk and reveal their attitudes and motivation. Listen to your customers. You can also keep abreast of purchasing patterns by observing competitors' practices and by asking sales personnel who is buying what, where.

Articles in business and trade newspapers and magazines give information on products, trends, marketing, finance, the economy. Trade directories, Yellow Pages, and brokers' direct-mail lists identify who buyers are, and most industries have associations and specialized marketing research that provide insights for understanding customers.

9. How to Promote Your Business (Idea List)

Here is a small business promotion strategies Idea List:

Perform an Advertising Promotion by Advertising in the classified advertising section of your community newspaper

Advertise in the Yellow Pages.

Advertise on a grocery buggy.

Another Business Promotional Idea is to approach your prospective customers over the phone.

Approach your prospective customers in person.

Approach your prospective customers through the mail.

Be a guest speaker at seminars and present on your area of expertise.

Be a guest speaker on radio talk shows.

Build and maintain a customer mailing and contact list on database software.

Build your image with well designed letterhead and business cards.

Design a brochure that best explains the benefits of your services.

Design a mail order promotion campaign.

Design a point of purchase display for your product.

Design a telemarketing promotional campaign.

Design an image building logo for your company.

Design and distribute a quarterly newsletter or an industry update announcement.

Design and distribute company calendars, mugs, pens, note pads, or other advertising specialties displaying your company name and logo.

Design and distribute a free "how to do it" hand-out related to your industry (e.g. Tips for conserving energy in your home).

Design buttons, decals and bumper stickers or balloons with your company name, logo or slogan.

Design T-shirts displaying your company name and logo.

Explore cross promotion with a non-competing company selling to your target market.

Explore the costs of advertising in newspapers, magazines, on radio, television, billboards, bus shelters and benches.

Explore ways to share your advertising costs using cooperative advertising.

Follow up customer purchases with a thank you letter.

Follow up customer purchases with Christmas or birthday cards.

Have your company profiled in a magazine or newspaper that is read by prospective customers.

Hire an advertising agency or public relations firm.

Hold a promotional contest.

Hold a seminar on your service, product or industry.

Include promotional material with your invoices.

Look for prospective customers at trade shows related to your industry.

Look for prospective customers in associations related to your industry.

Look for prospective customers at seminars related to your industry.

Look for prospective customers in magazines and newspapers related to your industry.

Package your brochure, price lists and letter in a folder for your customers.

Place a sidewalk sign outside your store or office.

Place flyers on bulletin boards and car windshields.

Place promotional notes on your envelopes, mailing labels.

Place signs or paint logos on your company vehicle(s).

Prepare a corporate video.

Prepare a list of product features and benefits to help you plan your advertising and promotional campaigns.

Prepare proposals offering solutions to your customers' needs

Provide free samples of your product or service.

Provide public tours of your operation.

Sponsor a charity event.

Sponsor an amateur sports team.

Sponsor a cultural event through a community arts organization.

10. Special Free Bonuses (download links are provided)

a. Excel Financial Projections Creator - simply type in your business' details and assumptions and it will automatically produce a comprehensive set of financial projections for your specific business, including: Start-Up Expenses, Projected Balance Sheet, Projected Cash Flow Statement, Financial Ratios Analysis, Projected Profit and Loss Statement, Break Even Analysis, and many more.

Copy the following link to your browser and save the file to your PC:

http://www.bizmove.com/bp/projections.xlsx

b. Detailed guide that will walk you step by step and show you exactly how to effectively use the above Excel Financial Projections Creator.

Copy the following link to your browser and save the file to your PC:

http://www.bizmove.com/bp/projections-guide.doc

c. How to Improve Your Leadership and Management Skills (eBook) - Discover powerful strategies to motivate and inspire your people to bring out the best in them. Be the boss people want to give 200 percent for.

Copy the following link to your browser and save the file to your PC:

http://www.bizmove.com/bp/leadership.pdf

d. Small Business Management: Essential Ingredients for Success (eBook) - Learn effective business management tricks, secrets and shortcuts to make your business a success.

Copy the following link to your browser and save the file to your PC:

http://www.bizmove.com/bp/management.pdf